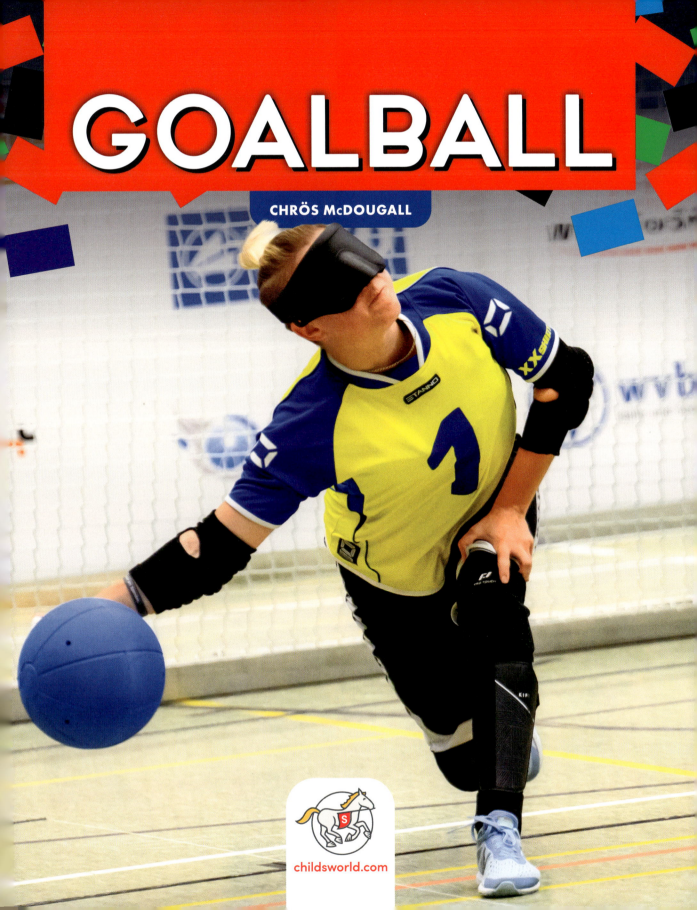
GOALBALL

CHRÖS McDOUGALL

Published by The Child's World®
800-599-READ • www.childsworld.com

Copyright © 2024 by The Child's World®
All rights reserved. No part of this book may be reproduced or utilized in any form or by any means without written permission from the publisher.

Photography Credits
Photographs ©: Jonas Walzberg/picture-alliance/dpa/AP Images, cover, 1; Shutterstock Images, 2, 6, 7, 12; Moto Yoshimura/Getty Images Sport/Getty Images, 3 (top), 19; Kiyoshi Ota/Getty Images Sport/Getty Images, 3 (bottom), 5; Dennis Grombkowski/Getty Images Sport/Getty Images, 9; iStockphoto, 11; Atsushi Tomura/Getty Images for Tokyo 2020/Getty Images Sport/Getty Images, 13; Alex Pantling/Getty Images Sport/Getty Images, 15, 17; Scott Heavey/Getty Images Sport/Getty Images, 18; Lintao Zhang/Getty Images Sport/Getty Images, 20, 21

ISBN Information
9781503885110 (Reinforced Library Binding)
9781503885714 (Portable Document Format)
9781503886353 (Online Multi-user eBook)
9781503886995 (Electronic Publication)

LCCN 2023937282

Printed in the United States of America

ABOUT THE AUTHOR

Chrös McDougall is an author, book editor, and sportswriter who has written several books for kids. He also covers Olympic and Paralympic sports for TeamUSA.org and other outlets. He lives in Minneapolis, Minnesota, with his wife, two kids, and a sleepy brindle Boxer named Eira.

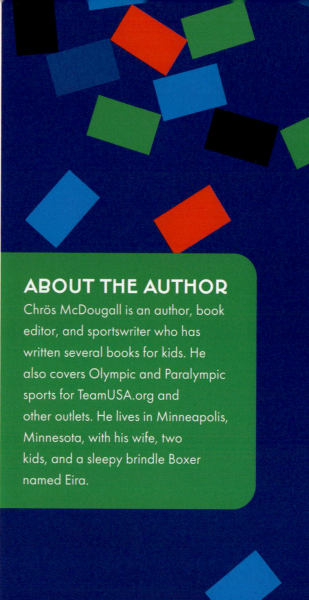

CONTENTS

CHAPTER ONE
GOING FOR THE GOAL . . . 4

CHAPTER TWO
ORIGINS OF THE GAME . . . 10

CHAPTER THREE
GOALBALL GREATS . . . 16

Glossary . . . 22

Fast Facts . . . 23

One Stride Further . . . 23

Find Out More . . . 24

Index . . . 24

CHAPTER ONE

GOING FOR THE GOAL

Val knelt and listened intently. The large gymnasium was quiet. In the distance, she heard shuffling feet. Then she heard a thud. Suddenly, the sound of small bells was barreling toward her.

In an instant, Val dove to her left. She hit the floor just in time to feel a thump on her outstretched arms. Immediately she gripped the hard rubber ball in her hands. Her teammates on the Tigers let out a cheer. But Val was already on her feet. She had ten seconds to send the ball back toward the other end of the court.

The Tigers were playing against a team called the Sharks. With less than a minute left in the game, the teams were tied 6–6. Val's team needed a goal to avoid overtime. The goalball regional championship was on the line.

Val cradled the ball in her hands. She listened for hints of where her opponents might be positioned. Then she went for it.

Goalball players often dive across the floor to prevent the other team from scoring.

Val took three steps forward before turning around. Holding the ball with both hands, she whipped it between her legs.

The ball bounced as it flew down the court. Val listened as her opponents scrambled. Finally, she heard a swish. Goal! The ball had rolled past the three Sharks on the other end of the court and gone into their net. That put the Tigers up 7–6. The Sharks had time for one more throw, but Val's teammate Becky stopped it with her outstretched feet. Then the buzzer sounded. The Tigers had won the championship!

Goalball is a team sport for athletes with visual impairments. It is played on a court approximately the same size as a volleyball court. Two teams of three line up on opposite ends of the floor. Over the course of a game, they take turns attacking. A player from the attacking team throws the ball across the court. The defenders try to block the ball any way they can. A team scores by sending the ball past the defenders and into a net that extends the width of the court. Whoever has more points at the end of the game wins.

Players often take a big windup before throwing the ball. Speed and bounce help the ball to get past the opponents.

COURT DIAGRAM

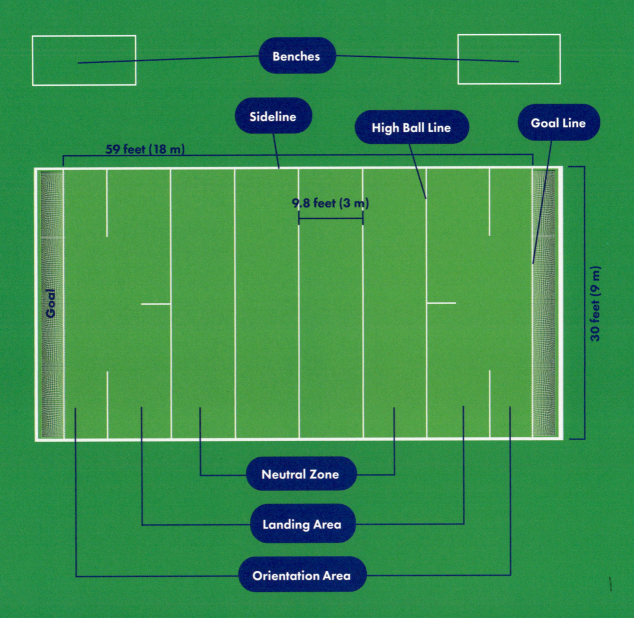

A shot must touch that team's landing area and the neutral zone as it travels toward the opponent's goal.

Scoring is harder than it sounds. Goalball players must wear **eyeshades**. These ensure that everyone has zero vision. Players try to track the 2.75-pound (1.25 kg) ball by sound. Small bells inside the ball ring when it moves. Raised lines on the court help the players know where they are positioned.

A court is divided into six zones. When a player throws the ball, it must touch that team's landing area and the neutral zone. Besides that, players can throw using whichever technique they prefer. Throws can be bouncing or rolling, and often throwers add spin to the ball so its path curves. At the Paralympics, throws reach speeds of around 35 miles per hour (56 kmh). But accuracy and strategy are key as well. Defenders use teamwork to get into position. Quick reactions are important. So is a willingness to dive across the court to stop the ball. Because the players rely on hearing the ball, crowds must be silent when a team is throwing.

A goalball game consists of two 12-minute halves. If the score remains tied, the game goes to overtime. Teams have two three-minute periods to try to score. If neither team scores, a **shootout** follows to determine the winner. And if a 10-point goal difference is reached during regulation time, a **mercy** is called. Then the leading team is declared the winner.

Goalball players must be willing to lay their bodies on the line to make a save.

CHAPTER TWO

ORIGINS OF THE GAME

After World War II (1939–1945), many soldiers came home with injuries. Sports were mostly designed for nondisabled people. This made it difficult for people with disabilities to participate. **Adaptive sports** provided them with opportunities.

Hans Lorenzen and Sepp Reindle worked with injured **veterans** in Europe. They noticed a problem. Many adaptive sports were for people with disabilities affecting their movement. But Lorenzen and Reindle also worked with patients who had trouble seeing. Some were blind. Lorenzen and Reindle sought an activity for these people. In 1946, they invented goalball.

The sport was originally played to help with **rehabilitation**. Over the years, it became more competitive. Athletes from around the world played, and the players wanted to win.

Some specialized equipment is needed to take part in a goalball game. That starts with the ball. It is round and made of hard blue rubber. It has a 9.8-inch (25 cm) **diameter**.

Wounded veterans sometimes use Para sports to help with rehabilitation.

Eyeshades ensure that goalball players have their vision completely blocked during games.

Small bells inside create sound. The game can be played in any gym that also hosts basketball or volleyball. However, special goals and court markings are needed. At major tournaments, players must wear matching uniforms. This includes a jersey, trousers, and socks. Many players also wear padding for extra protection. In addition, eyeshades are required for all players.

Goalball was one of many adaptive sports to take off after World War II. In 1960, a competition was held in Rome, Italy. Eight sports were played. More than 400 athletes from 23 countries took part. Organizers called it the Paralympic Games.

Players defending against a shot listen for the bells inside the ball as well as the bounce of the ball to know where it is going. ▶

The Paralympics are now held every four years, just a few weeks after the Olympics. Goalball was not part of the first Paralympics. The sport first appeared in the Games in 1972. However, it was a demonstration event, meaning no medals were awarded. Men's goalball became a medal sport four years later. A women's event was added in 1984.

The Paralympic gold medal remains the sport of goalball's biggest prize. However, top players now have other important competitions. The biggest of them is the World Championships. The first World Championships in 1978 was just for men, with women joining for the next edition in 1982. Like the Paralympics, the competition is held every four years.

Countries around the world play goalball. In 2021, the Paralympics were held in Tokyo, Japan. Brazil won the men's gold medal. In 12 Paralympics, ten countries had won the men's gold. Only Finland in 1996 and 2012, and Denmark in 2000 and 2004, had won multiple titles.

THE PARALYMPIC MOVEMENT

Paralympic combines the words *para* and *Olympic*. In Greek, *para* roughly means "alongside." The name reflects that the Paralympics exist alongside the Olympics. Both are held every four years. Each has a Summer and Winter Games. Each Summer Games has used the same host city since 1988, while the Winter Games has shared hosts since 1992.

The US women's goalball team celebrates its first-round victory over Brazil at the Tokyo Paralympic Games in 2021.

On the women's side, Turkey successfully defended its gold medal in 2021. That made Turkey the third country to win two golds in women's goalball. Canada also won back-to-back in 2000 and 2004. The United States won in 1984 and 2008.

CHAPTER THREE

GOALBALL GREATS

Amanda Dennis was born with two **genetic conditions**. Though she has some vision, she is legally blind. Growing up in Georgia, Dennis started playing goalball at age seven. She grew into one of the world's best players. At 27, she was already competing in her third Paralympics for the United States.

Dennis played in the center position on defense. That is the most important position on a team. But on offense, she was known for her fast and twisting throws, which made her a dangerous scorer. In 2021, the US women reached the Paralympic semifinal in Tokyo, Japan. With two and a half minutes remaining, Brazil led 2–0. But the ball was in Dennis's hands. She stepped forward and spun in a full circle, then released a strong, bouncing throw like a bowler toward the opposing net. Two diving Brazil players tried to stop it. Instead, the ball slipped between them and into the net.

Team USA goalball star Amanda Dennis displays the USA flag on her eyeshades as she competes against Brazil during the Paralympic Games in 2021.

Team USA still needed one more goal. Then, with 18 seconds left, Dennis got the ball again. She lined up and threw as she had done before. But this time Dennis aimed her throw toward the near corner, fooling the defenders. Her goal tied the game 2–2. The Americans eventually won the game in a shootout. Some were already calling it one of the greatest games in goalball history.

THERE IS NO STOPPING THEM

Lisa Czechowski and Asya Miller became Paralympic teammates in 2000. Twenty-one years later, they competed in their sixth Games together for Team USA. The pair has won four goalball medals. Among them was a gold medal in 2008. But each one also won another Paralympic medal in 2000 in track and field.

Team USA ended up winning the silver medal in Tokyo. Dennis was injured and missed the final. Behind star player Sevda Altunoluk, Turkey cruised to a 9–2 win and claimed a second gold medal in a row.

Altunoluk was born in Tokat, a midsize city in central Turkey. She began the sport at age 12. With her aggressive throwing style, she became a dominant scorer. Nobody scored more goals at the Paralympics in 2016 or 2021. Among her 46 goals in Tokyo were eight in the final. Many consider her to be the world's best player.

Goalball players come from many backgrounds. At 39, Daryl Walker was the oldest member of the US Paralympic men's team in 2021. He learned about the sport in physical education class. Others learned of goalball through sports education camps. These are camps where kids with visual impairments can try many sports.

Turkey's Sevda Altunoluk celebrates a goal at the World Championships in 2022.

Daryl Walker dives to make a save for Team USA during the first round of the Paralympic Games in 2021.

Zach Buhler of Team USA makes a save against Brazil during the Tokyo Games in 2021.

Zach Buhler, John Kusku, Tyler Merren, and Matt Simpson found the sport this way. Outside of goalball, each works a full-time job. Simpson is a lawyer. Calahan Young is a **recreational therapist**. Merren works as a personal trainer. But when Team USA called, the six men came together. In Tokyo, they reached the bronze-medal game and finished fourth.

GLOSSARY

adaptive sports (uh-DAP-tiv SPORTS) Adaptive sports are competitive sports designed for people with disabilities. Goalball is one of many adaptive sports played at the Paralympic Games.

diameter (dye-AM-uh-tur) The diameter of an object is the length of a straight line through the center of it. The diameter of a goalball is 25 centimeters (approximately 10 inches).

eyeshades (EYE-shayds) Eyeshades are a piece of equipment that covers a player's eyes. All players use eyeshades while playing goalball.

genetic conditions (juh-NET-ik kuhn-DISH-uhns) Genetic conditions result when parents pass down a changed gene to their child, which puts the child at risk of developing a particular condition, such as a disability or illness. Blindness can be a genetic condition passed through someone's genes.

mercy (MUR-see) Mercy is a rule in sports where the game ends if one team is beating another team by a significant number of points during regulation time. In goalball, a mercy is called after a team is ahead by 10 points.

recreational therapist (rek-ree-AY-shun-uhl THAYR-uh-pist) A recreational therapist is a health care provider who uses activity-based techniques to help people with injuries, illnesses, or disabilities. The recreational therapist helped the veteran rehabilitate.

rehabilitation (re-huh-bil-uh-TAY-shun) Rehabilitation is the process of helping somebody regain physical function. The injured veterans had to go through rehabilitation.

shootout (SHOOT-out) Also called extra throws, a shootout is a tiebreaker after overtime to determine the winner. Teams take turns shooting one-on-one.

veterans (VET-ur-uhns) Veterans are people who served in the armed forces. Veterans use adaptive sports to rehabilitate from their injuries.

FAST FACTS

- Goalball was invented in Europe in 1946 by Hans Lorenzen and Sepp Reindle as an activity for injured veterans.

- In a game, teams of three try to send a ball past their opponents and across the goal line.

- The ball has bells inside so players can hear its movements. Players also wear eyeshades so no one is able to see.

- A men's goalball tournament was added to the Paralympic Games in 1976. A women's tournament followed in 1984.

- The Paralympic gold medal is the sport's biggest prize. The World Championships are another important tournament. Both are held every four years.

- At the Paralympics in 2021, Amanda Dennis scored two goals in the final 2:28 of the semifinal to help the US women come back from being down 2–0 and advance to the gold-medal game.

- Sevda Altunoluk led Turkey's women's team to Paralympic gold medals in 2016 and 2021. She was the tournament's leading scorer both times.

ONE STRIDE FURTHER

- What are some qualities that would make a good goalball player?

- Why is it important to have sports for people with visual impairments?

- How would you throw the ball? Why do you think that would be an effective method?

FIND OUT MORE

IN THE LIBRARY

Alexander, Lori. *A Sporting Chance: How Ludwig Guttmann Created the Paralympic Games.* Boston, MA: Houghton Mifflin Harcourt, 2020.

Herman, Gail. *What Are the Paralympic Games?* New York, NY: Penguin Workshop, 2020.

Mason, Paul. *Paralympic Power.* London, UK: Wayland, 2019.

ON THE WEB

Visit our website for links about goalball:
childsworld.com/links

Note to Parents, Caregivers, Teachers, and Librarians: We routinely verify our Web links to make sure they are safe and active sites. So encourage your readers to check them out!

INDEX

Altunoluk, Sevda, 18

Buhler, Zach, 21

Czechowski, Lisa, 18

Dennis, Amanda, 16–18

Kusku, John, 21

Lorenzen, Hans, 10

Merren, Tyler, 21
Miller, Asya, 18

Reindle, Sepp, 10

Simpson, Matt, 21

Walker, Daryl, 18
World Championships, 14
World War II, 10, 12

Young, Calahan, 21